ALL ROUND ENGLISH 2

Ronald Ridout
and Michael Holt

Illustrated
by
Joseph
Wright

Longman

STEP 1

A True or false?

Scatty wrote eleven sentences about the picture at the top right. Poor Scatty didn't think very carefully what he was writing. Five of his sentences are quite false.
Can you spot them?
Write out the six sentences that are true.

The girl is higher up than the boy.
The boy is lower down than the girl.
The dog has more legs than the bird.
The cat has more tails than the dog.
The cyclist is going faster than the dog.
The cyclist is younger than the girl.
The dog is running after the cat.
The cat and the dog
    have eight legs all together.
The boy is fishing for sharks.
The cat will get to the river ford
    before the cyclist.
The cyclist's brakes don't work
    and he will get wet.

B Sentences

When you copied the sentences in A, you began each with a capital letter and ended each with a full stop.

The dog is running after the cat.

↑ capital letter   ↑ full stop

Write out the sentences on the right.
Complete each with one of these words:

| first | moon | yellow | hedges |
| space | right | cotton | two |

1 When they are ripe, bananas go __.
2 The __ goes round the earth.
3 A bicycle has __ wheels.
4 January is the __ month of the year.
5 Most people throw with their __ arm.
6 We clip __ with shears.
7 Jeans are usually made of __.
8 Gagarin was the first person to orbit
    the earth in __.

C Choose aright

Choose the right verb and then write out the sentence.

1 Cats purr, but dogs (sing, bark, bray).
2 Sheep (bleat, bark, quack), but pigs grunt.
3 Ducks waddle, but horses (hop, crawl, trot).
4 Motorists (walk, drive, gallop), but cyclists ride.
5 Stars twinkle, but the sun (speaks, eats, shines).
6 We (eat, see, smell) with our noses, but we hear with our ears.

D Containers

We put something in each of these things.

1 a purse   3 a wardrobe   5 the larder
2 a vase   4 a kettle   6 envelopes

Say what we put in each thing. Begin like this:

1 **We** put money in a purse.

This is what we keep in them:

clothes	food	water
money	letters	flowers

E Very short sentences

What do these things do?

1 clocks   3 bees   5 the wind
2 doors   4 ships   6 a ball

Write sentences to say what they do.
Begin like this: 1 Clocks tick.

This is what they do:

blows	sail	open
buzz	bounces	tick

F Make your own sentences

Say what these do:

1 bands   3 a duck   5 knives
2 stars   4 the sun   6 a mouse

G About yourself

1 I get up every morning
  at half past seven.
2 At eight o'clock I have breakfast.
3 I set off for school at quarter to nine.
4 School begins at nine o'clock.
5 We have a short break at half past ten.
6 Morning school finishes
  at half past twelve.

7 I have lunch in the school canteen.
8 We start school again at two o'clock.
9 We go home at four o'clock.
10 After tea I play or watch television.
11 I am supposed to go to bed
   at eight o'clock.

Stephen Hill wrote these sentences.
Copy them, but make them true for you.

3

STEP 2

a moth   a spanner   a key

ABCDEFGHIJKLMNOPQRSTUVWXYZ

a b c d ef g h i jk l mn o pq r st u v w x yz

A The alphabet

Here are some sentences about the alphabet. There is one word missing from each sentence.

Complete the sentences by choosing the right word from the list. But beware! There are two words in the list that you don't need.

between	capital	first
no	last	twenty-six
two	before	alphabet
four	three	twenty-four

1 The __ letter of the alphabet is A.
2 The __ letter of the alphabet is Z.
3 The letter K comes __ J and L.
4 There are only __ letters after X.
5 The letter D comes __ E but after C.
6 There are — letters between B and F.
7 The second letter of the __ is B.
8 E G J M are four __ letters.
9 There are __ letters after Z.

B Alphabet sentences

Acrobat begins with A.
Banana begins with B.
Canoe   begins with C.
Dragon . . .

Can you finish this list of alphabet sentences? Write one sentence for each letter of the alphabet.

To make sure you spell the words correctly, find your words in the Little Dictionary. You can also use the words in the picture.

C Who married whom?

All these girls married boys whose names began with the same letter as theirs.
Who, then, married whom? Take them in alphabetical order. Begin like this:

1 Angela married Alan.
2 Brenda . . .

Carole	Fred
Emma	Alan
Helen	Geoffrey
Angela	Barry
Gillian	Edward
Diana	Charles
Frances	Harold
Brenda	David

D Alphabetical order

Look at the two lists of words on the right.
What is the difference between them?
Yes, the second one is in alphabetical order,
but the first one isn't. In the alphabetical
list <u>actor</u> comes before <u>clown</u> because <u>a</u> comes
before <u>c</u> in the alphabet. In the same
way, <u>guard</u> comes before <u>manager</u>
because <u>g</u> comes before <u>m</u>.

But why does <u>manager</u> come before <u>motorist</u>?
When two words begin with the same letter,
we must look at the second letter. <u>Manager</u>
comes before <u>motorist</u> because <u>a</u> comes before <u>o</u>.
In the same way <u>sentry</u> comes before <u>soldier</u>
because <u>e</u> comes before <u>o</u>.

sentry
clown
motorist
soldier
actor
manager
guard

actor
clown
guard
manager
motorist
sentry
soldier

Write each of these lists in alphabetical order.

1	2	3	4	5	6
monkey	nurse	pilot	large	Wayne	Spain
donkey	doctor	soldier	small	Kate	Brazil
lion	farmer	policeman	fat	Wendy	Sweden
horse	dentist	sailor	thin	Kevin	Belgium
giraffe	engineer	jockey	slim	Sarah	China
cat	artist	miner	tall	Simon	Canada

E Top and tail alike

Copy this puzzle and solve it with the help of the clues.
Check your answers with the Little Dictionary at the end of the book.

1	P			P	
2	T			T	
3	K			K	
4	F			F	
5	R			R	
6	S				S
7	W			W	
8	E				E

CLUES

1 Fat and chubby.
2 The opposite of loose.
3 A light canoe used by Eskimos.
4 The soft feathery stuff that comes from blankets.
5 Men shave with this.
6 You can cut hedges with these.
7 A woman who has lost her husband.
8 You say this at the end if you want the actors to do it again.

5

STEP 3

SCATTY Hello! Hello!

LIZ Who's that?

SCATTY It's me.

LIZ Yes, but what's your name?

SCATTY I'm Scatty.

LIZ Oh, it's you again, is it?

SCATTY Yes, it's me.
Hello! Hello!
I'm Scatty, I'm Scatty.
I'm not Ted, I'm not Dick.
I'm not Fred, I'm not Nick.
I'm Scatty. That's me.
Good-bye! Good-bye!

LIZ No, don't go. Now you're here you can answer some more questions. Miss Lee has given us a whole list to answer. So let's begin. First, what is your name?

SCATTY I'm Scatty, I'm Scatty.
I'm not Ted. I'm not . . .

LIZ All right! That's enough. Here's the next one. How old are you?

SCATTY I'm a hundred.

LIZ I don't believe you. I'll put you down as ten. Next, how many brothers and sisters have you?

SCATTY I haven't any.

LIZ Right. Well done, Scatty. (He bows.) Here's another. Where do you live?

SCATTY I live at Number 19, New Road.

LIZ That's right too. Your English is improving fast, Scatty.

KEVIN Yes, it is, isn't it?

LIZ Oh, it was you answering all the time. I thought it was odd.

KEVIN Ha! ha! Ha! ha!
I'm Kevin, I'm Kevin.
I'm not Ted, I'm not Dick.
I'm not Fred, I'm not Nick.
I'm Kevin. That's me.
Good-bye! Good-bye!

A Questions and answers

Copy the questions and choose the best answer for each from the list below.

1 When is Boxing Day?
2 Do you spell BUZZ with a double Z?
3 Where is Cardiff?
4 Who first sailed round the world?
5 What is Scatty?

It is in South Wales.
He is a puppet.
Yes, you do.
It is on 26th December.
Magellan did.

B Question sentences

Look at this question sentence:

What is Scatty?

capital letter   question mark

(W)   (?)

Question sentences begin with a capital letter and end with a question mark.

Here are some sentences that Scatty wrote. *Correct them and show him how to write them out properly.*

1 what is your name
2 where is New York
3 who first crossed the Atlantic by air
4 do you like swimming
5 when is your birthday
6 are there any more questions

C Various questions

Here are 8 very different questions.

Write out each question and find the answer for it in the other list.

QUESTIONS	ANSWERS
1 Is Scatty a puppet?	Liz is.
2 Is he really a hundred years old?	He lives at 19 New Road.
3 Where does he live?	Yes, he did.
4 What is Kevin doing in the picture?	Yes, he is.
5 Who is talking to Scatty in the picture?	It is the seventh.
6 Did Kevin or Scatty sing the last song?	He is hiding under the table.
7 Is this the sixth question or the seventh?	Kevin sang it.
8 Did Kevin answer for Scatty?	No, he isn't.

D Answer these yourself

1 Are you a boy or a girl?
2 What is your full name?
3 How old are you?
4 What colour are your eyes?
5 What are you writing with?
6 Where do you live?
7 What is your favourite game?

Have you remembered the capital letter and the full stop?

Yes, I have.

Scatty

E Alphabetical order

Arrange each of these lists in alphabetical order.

1 Kevin, Scatty, Liz, Steve, Leslie, Karen
2 birds, deer, bees, animals, dragons, alligators
3 Morgan, Phillips, Mitchell, Norton, Nixon, Parker
4 London, Birmingham, Liverpool, Bristol, Edinburgh, Exeter

STEP 4

A What can you see?

The words in the list name the garments hanging on the line. But watch out! Some other things that are not on the line are named too.

Write out only the names of the five garments you can see on the line.

a shirt	a coat	a pair of jeans
a vest	a hat	a pair of socks
a dress	a pullover	a pair of pyjamas

B In order

Now write five sentences to say what there is hanging on the line. Make sure you get the order right.

Begin your sentences like this:
1 First there is a pair of socks on the line.
2 Then there is . . .
3 Next . . .
4 After that . . .
5 Last of all . . .

C Hanging up

Mrs Smith hung up the clothes on the line. She hung up the pair of jeans first, and last of all she hung up the pair of socks.

Write five more sentences to say which order she hung them up in.
Use First . . . Then . . . Next . . .
After that . . . Last of all . . .

D Taking down

Now imagine another line. There are five things hanging on it, and Scatty is just going to take them down.
Write five sentences to tell us the order in which he is going to take them down.

Begin like this:
1 First Scatty is going to take down the towel.

1 a towel	3 a blanket	5 a table cloth
2 a sheet	4 a curtain	

E Nouns

Nouns name things, as this diagram shows:

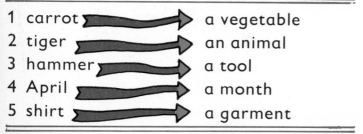

1	carrot	→	a vegetable
2	tiger	→	an animal
3	hammer	→	a tool
4	April	→	a month
5	shirt	→	a garment

Now write out the five sentences, like this:

1 Carrot is the name of a vegetable.

F What do they name?

These nouns are the names of the things in the second list. *Say what each is the name of. Begin like this:*

1 Eagle is the name of a bird.

1 eagle	4 Monday	7 tea
2 ant	5 rose	8 France
3 potato	6 woman	9 shark

day	country	flower
drink	vegetable	insect
bird	fish	person

G Classes

Here are 15 more nouns. An equal number of them name vegetables, drinks and flowers. *Write them out in three groups, like this:*

1 VEGETABLES: cabbage, carrot . . .

2 DRINKS:

3 FLOWERS:

rose	tea	daisy	peas	beer
cabbage	tulip	lettuce	wine	primrose
carrot	coffee	lemonade	pansy	beans

H Using the dictionary

We say in **F** that an eagle is a bird; an ant is an insect; a potato is a vegetable; tea is a drink; etc. Below are some more nouns.

Can you say what they name? Use the Little Dictionary to find out or check your answers. Begin like this:

1 An igloo is a kind of house built of snow.

1 an igloo	3 a mallet	5 a walrus
2 a kayak	4 a banjo	6 an egret

I Draw and write

Here are some more nouns. You probably know the things they name. But what can you do with them? *Draw the things and under each one write a sentence to say what you can do with it.*

1 a mask	3 a telescope	5 a saw
2 a penknife	4 a football	6 scissors

This is a mask. I can see fish and strange beautiful shells under the sea with it.

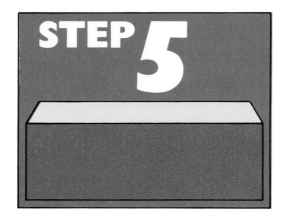

STEP 5

angler, a person who fishes with a line
barber, a man who cuts hair and shaves
chemist, a person who sells medicines
cyclist, a person who rides a bicycle
decorator, a man who paints
    and repairs houses
fireman, a man who fights fires
giant, anyone of huge size
glider, an aircraft without an engine
hose, a long narrow pliable pipe
    to bring water from a distance
mirror, a piece of glass in which we can
    see ourselves
muzzle, the open end of a gun
nephew, the son of your brother
    or sister

A The dictionary

The list at the top on the right shows
you how words are listed in a dictionary.
They are arranged in alphabetical order
so that you can quickly find the word
you want.

*With the help of the list, find the missing
words to complete each of these sentences:*

1 A man who fights fires is called a __.
2 An angler fishes with a __.
3 Cyclists ride __.
4 The open end of a gun is called its __.
5 The son of a man's sister is his __.
6 We can see __ when we look in a mirror.
7 Giants are __ people.
8 You can buy __ at the chemist's shop.

B Using the dictionary

*Find these nouns in the Little Dictionary at
the end of the book. What do they name?
Write them out in alphabetical order with
their meanings, as in the list at the top right.*

nest	stream	butcher
pianist	dwarf	camera

C Use the dictionary again

*Now look these nouns up in the Little
Dictionary. Explain the meaning of each
word in a sentence, like this:*

1 A poacher is a person who steals
  animals from someone's land.

1 poacher	3 groom	5 motorist
2 restaurant	4 plough	6 acrobat

D Alphabetical order

*Arrange each of these lists of nouns in
alphabetical order.*

1 rug	2 goose	3 pistol
rifle	glider	poison
rock	garage	person
referee	guest	passenger
raft	giant	pudding
rhino	grass	platform

E A story

Here is a story, but instead of the noun there is sometimes a picture of the thing named by the noun. *Write out the story, putting the right nouns instead of the pictures. Choose from this list.*

cows   church
field   school
gate   bus stop
Kevin   houses
shop   road

Kevin walks to every morning. On his way he passes a .

Beyond the church there is a large . Sometimes there are

 in the field. After the field there is a row of 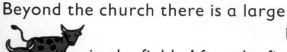.

At the end of the row there is a . Then there is a .

A few yards farther on, the 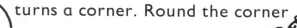 turns a corner. Round the corner

can see his school. He goes into the school through a big iron.

F Wendy's story

This is a picture map of Wendy's walk to Kate's house. *Write some sentences to say what she passes or sees on the way to her friend.*

G A word game

The first player begins by saying: I went to the supermarket and bought an axe. The second player repeats this and adds the name of something beginning with B. And so on. The fifth player might have to say: I went to the supermarket and bought an axe, some biscuits, a chicken, some dates and an egg-whisk.

Any player who gets the order wrong or adds something beginning with the wrong letter drops out.

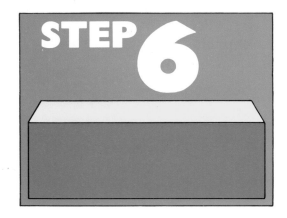

Name	Age
John	8
Ann	7
Simon	10
Kate	8
James	7
Sarah	6

A Answer the questions
Begin like this:

1 He is seven **years old.**

1 How old is the youngest boy?
2 How old is Ann?
3 How old is the oldest child?
4 How old is the youngest girl?
5 How old is the oldest girl?
6 How old will James be in a year's time?
7 How old was Kate a year ago?
8 How old is the boy who is two years older than Kate?

B Which is?
Begin like this:

1 Simon is.

1 Which of the six children is the oldest?
2 Which of them is the youngest?
3 Which of the boys is younger than Kate?
4 Which of the girls is the youngest?
5 Which of the boys is seven years old?
6 Which two children are eight?
7 Which of the girls is older than James?
8 Which of the children is the same age as Ann?

C Various questions
1 Is John the oldest of the boys?
2 How many of the girls are eight?
3 How many of the boys are only six?
4 How old was Simon three years ago?
5 How many of the children are seven?
6 How many of the boys are older than Ann?
7 Are any of the girls nine yet?
8 Was Ann six a year ago?
9 How many of the children were under six two years ago?
10 Which of the children will be ten in three years time?

D   Ask the three girls how old they were a year ago, and ask the three boys how old they were two years ago. Begin like this:

1   YOU How old were you a year ago, Ann?
    ANN I was six.

E   Ask the three boys how old they will be in a year's time, and ask the three girls how old they will be in two years time. Begin like this:

1   YOU How old will you be in a year's time, John?
    JOHN I shall be nine.

F   Choose the right words to complete the sentences. Then write them out.

1 James is older than __. (Kate, John, Sarah)
2 Kate is a year older than __. (Sarah, Ann, John)
3 __ will be ten in two years time. (John, Simon, Kate)
4 Ann is younger than __. (Sarah, Kate, James)
5 __ was only five a year ago. (Sarah, John, Ann)
6 John is older than both __ and __. (Ann, James, Kate)

G   Ask other pupils the nine questions you can make from this table. Gary's birthday is on 23rd July. This is how he replied when he was asked the first question:

1 DICK Are you as old as Fiona, who will be nine on 14th May?
   GARY Yes, I am slightly older than she is.

Are you as old as	Fiona, who will be nine on 14th May?
Are you older than	the pupil sitting next to you?
Are you younger than	Tom, who was eight on 1st July?

H Ken wrote this:

I am eight years old. I shall be nine on 25th April. I am looking forward to that day because I always have a party on my birthday. Mum makes a huge cake with candles on it. I have to blow them all out at one go. Then my friends all sing "Happy birthday to you!"

Write about yourself in the same way as Ken did.

13

STEP 7

TOM   SALLY   KATE

WAYNE   LINDA   KEVIN

A Add the right sentence
Begin like this:

Tom was not riding a bicycle when
Mr Cooper took his photo.
He was riding a donkey.

1 Tom was not riding a bicycle when
  Mr Cooper took his photo. . . .
2 Sally was not climbing a ladder. . . .
3 Kate was not carrying a kitten. . . .
4 Wayne was not pulling a rope. . . .
5 Linda was not pushing a pram. . . .
6 Kevin was not throwing a ball. . . .

B Who was?
*Answer these questions with short complete
sentences. Begin like this:*

1 Wayne was.

1 Who was pulling a hose-pipe when Mr
  Cooper took his photo?
2 Who was throwing a dart?
3 Who was riding a donkey?
4 Who was carrying a puppy?
5 Who was pushing her bicycle?
6 Who was climbing a tree?

Tom   Sally   Kate
Wayne   Linda   Kevin

C What were you doing?
*Ask the children what they were doing
when Mr Cooper took their photos, like this:*

1 YOU What were you doing when
        Mr Cooper took your photo, Tom?
  TOM I was riding a donkey.

D A frightened donkey
*Choose one of the children in the photos and
say what he or she did after Mr Cooper had
taken the photo. This is how Peter began:*

After Mr Cooper had taken his photo,
Tom rode the donkey along the beach.
A boy waved a flag at him. The donkey
was so frightened that it galloped off . . .

E Verbs

When their photos were taken, the children were all performing actions. Tom was riding, Sally was climbing, Kate was carrying, Wayne was pulling, Linda was pushing, and Kevin was throwing. Words that tell us the action are called verbs. Was riding, was climbing, was carrying, etc., are all verbs.

There are 12 more verbs in this list.
Set them out alphabetically as in a dictionary.

bloom, to come into flower
explain, to make clear
correct, to put right
halt, to stop walking
grab, to seize quickly with the hands
chew, to break up with the teeth
guard, to watch over; to protect
cycle, to ride a bicycle
bake, to cook in an oven
float, to stay on the surface of the water
announce, to make something known
accompany, to go with

F One word for several

Study the verbs and their meanings in the list. Then use one of the verbs to replace the underlined part of each of the sentences. Begin like this:

1 We always cycle to school.

1 We always ride our bicycles to school.
2 Daffodils come into flower in April.
3 Wendy doesn't know the way to the library so Jane is going to go with her.
4 Colin can swim, and now he is learning to stay on the surface of the water.
5 Please watch over my clothes while I have a swim.
6 Put right your mistakes before you do anything else.

G Using the dictionary

Look up these verbs in the Little Dictionary, and then write them out alphabetically with their meanings.

scald	juggle	imprison
faint	ascend	forsake
injure	upset	chatter

H A word game

The first player says: When I reached the park Andrew was acting. The next player repeats this and adds the name of a boy or girl whose name begins with B and who was doing something beginning with B. And so on. The fifth player might say: When I reached the park, Andrew was acting, Brian was batting, Christine was climbing, Diana was diving, and Eric was eating.

STEP 8

A What's his line?

Kevin has decided to be a docker and the other children are trying to find out what he is by asking him questions that he can answer with Yes or No.
Answer these questions with Yes or No?
Begin like this:

1 No, he doesn't.

1 Does a docker work in a factory?
2 Does he work in the open air?
3 Does he work near the sea?
4 Does he work in an office?
5 Does he carry things?
6 Does he load and unload boats?

Q Do you work in an office?
A No, I don't.
Q Do you work in a factory?
A No, I don't.
Q Do you work out-of-doors?
A Yes, I do.
Q Do you grow things?
A No, I don't.
Q Do you work on the sea?
A No, I don't.
Q Do you work near the sea?
A Yes, I do.
Q Do you make boats?
A No, I don't.
Q Do you carry things?
A Yes, I do.
Q Do you unload boats?
A Yes, I do.
Q Are you a docker?
A Yes, I am.

B Making sentences

Make 6 sentences by giving each beginning its right ending.

1 Seamen   fuel the boilers.
2 The captain   controls the seamen.
3 Stokers   steers the ship.
4 The cook   work on ships.
5 The boatswain   feeds those on board.
6 The helmsman   commands the ship.

C Can you guess?

1 He has a shop. He sells, beef, mutton, pork, liver and sausages. What is he?
2 He is in charge of an airliner. He steers it and brings it down to land. What is he?
3 He works in a garage. He services cars and repairs them. What is he?
4 He reads the news on television. What is he called?

D Making up riddles

Make up five more riddles about people,
like those in **C**—*about a pop singer,*
a plumber, a jockey, a racing motorist,
a nurse, an acrobat, or anyone you like
to choose.

E What do they do?

Look these nouns up in the Little Dictionary.
Then write a sentence to say what each
person named by the noun does. Begin like
this:

1 A groom looks after horses.

1 a groom   3 a potter   5 a stationer
2 a surgeon   4 a fiddler   6 a spectator

F The missing noun

With the help of the Little Dictionary,
find the name that is missing from each
of these sentences:

1 Dentists look after people's __.
2 An angler catches __.
3 Grooms rub down and feed __.
4 Florists sell __.
5 Bricklayers lay __.
6 A dramatist writes __.

G Nouns and verbs

Make 5 sentences by joining each verb to
the right noun.

1 Athletes   paint.
2 Artists   investigate.
3 Jockeys   learn.
4 Detectives   run.
5 Pupils   ride.

H Something to write about

Choose any person who does something
interesting, and write about what he or
she does. You could say what the person
does every day or you could write about
one special day. This is how Wendy
began:

A lighthouse keeper's job is interesting
because it is so different from anyone else's.
Just imagine it. He is out there day after day
with just one other member of the lighthouse
crew. They see nothing all day long except
an occasional ship passing. From morning
till night they hear nothing but the sea and
the wind.

I A game to play

Play the game of What's my Line? as Kevin
and the others played it.

STEP 9

Tom bought a gas-filled balloon at a fete last summer. He had a great deal of fun with it. Then the string slipped out of his hand. The balloon floated up into the air and he lost it.

We saw Tom's balloon in a good many different places. We have chosen six of the places and made a picture of each. Can you find all six pictures? They are numbered to show you the right order.

A Put them in the right order

These sentences tell you where the balloon was at various times, but they are in the wrong order. *Can you put them in the right order?*

Soon it was drifting across the river.

A few minutes later it was under Mrs Lee's sunshade.

Last of all, it was flying high up in the air.

At first Tom was holding the balloon behind his back.

After that it was flying over the church tower.

Then it was rising above him, beyond his reach.

B Answer the questions

1 Where was Tom holding the balloon at first?
2 Where was the balloon after that?
3 Where was it a few minutes later?
4 What was the balloon doing after that?
5 Where was it flying next?
6 What was it doing last of all?

C Tom's answers

We asked Tom these questions, and these were his answers.

1 Where do you sit in class? — I sit in the back row.
2 Where do you sit at lunch? — I usually sit next to Dick.
3 Where do you buy your sweets? — I usually buy them at the shop on the corner.
4 Where did you go last Sunday? — I went to Whipsnade Zoo.
5 Where are you going next week-end? — I am going to the seaside to swim.
6 Where would you like to go for your next summer holidays? — I should like to go to one of the islands in the West Indies.

How would you answer the same questions? Write your answers down.

D *Can you give each of these beginnings its right ending? If you do this correctly, you will make sentences that explain what a bakery, an orchard, etc., is.*

1 A bakery is a building   where clothes are kept.
2 An orchard is a field   where bread is baked.
3 A wardrobe is a cupboard   where the dead are buried.
4 A theatre is a building   where apples are grown.
5 A prison is a place   where aircraft land and take off.
6 A cemetery is a place   where clothes are washed and pressed.
7 A laundry is a building   where plays are performed.
8 An airport is a place   where criminals are kept.

⑤

⑥

E   If you want to know what we call a cupboard where clothes are kept, you ask a question like this:

1 YOU   What do we call a cupboard where clothes are kept, Ann?
    ANN   It is called a wardrobe.

Now ask someone what we call the following:

1 a building where bread is baked
2 a building where clothes are washed
3 a field where apples are grown
4 a place where aircraft land

5 a building where criminals are kept
6 a place where people are buried
7 a cupboard where clothes are kept
8 a building where plays are performed

F   *How quickly can you now finish this list?*
   Clothes are kept in a wardrobe. Bread is baked at a bakery. The dead are buried in a cemetery.

G Guided composition
Pretend that you saw Tom when he bought his balloon and watched it from start to finish. Tell a friend what happened. Mention all six places where you saw the balloon. Finish by saying something like this:
When I last saw that balloon it was flying high up in the sky. Tom had well and truly lost it.

H The moon by *J. M. Westrup*
Write a poem like this about the sun.
I saw the moon
One windy night
Flying so fast—
All silvery white—
Over the sky
Like a toy balloon
Loose from its string—
A run-away moon.

19

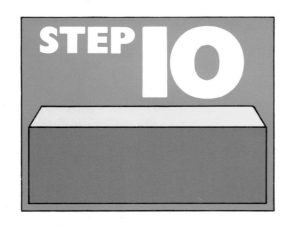

A Golden hamsters

No other pet has ever become popular as fast as the hamster has. Fifty years ago they were unknown. Today thousands have hamsters for pets.

One April morning in Syria, Professor Aronin was collecting wild animals. He stopped by a burrow and began to dig. At the end of a **170** centimetres tunnel he found a mother with twelve young in her nest.

He put the young ones in a cage and took them back to Jerusalem with him. Hamsters had never been kept in cages before. All of them died except for one male and two females. These ate well and grew fast. One of the females had a litter —the first hamsters ever born in a cage. All the hamsters in schools, pet shops and homes came from that first litter.

1 Judging from the picture, how long would you say a hamster is?
2 In what year roughly did Professor Aronin find his young hamsters?
3 How many metres long was the tunnel, very roughly—$\frac{1}{2}$ metre, 1 metre, 2 metres or 3 metres?
4 How many hamsters died?

B Something to draw

1 Draw a hamster twice as big as the one in the picture. Squared paper will help.
2 Draw the map of Syria twice as big. Make a scale for it.

TURKEY

ALEPPO
RAQQA
MEDITERRANEAN SEA
HAMA
S Y R I A
HOMS
O PALMYRA
LEBANON
DAMASCUS
IRAQ
ISRAEL
JERUSALEM
JORDAN

MILES
0   50   100
0   50   100
KILOMETRES

C Bar charts

This is a bar chart. It is a sort of graph. It shows facts about figures clearly, so that you can see the facts at a glance. This bar chart is about the hobbies of children in Sue's class. We can read the graph like this:

Ten of the children in Sue's class collect stamps.

Five of them collect 'tea cards'.

Seven go to Brownies or Cubs and three collect match-boxes.

How many children are there in Sue's class? None of the children had two hobbies. (Hint: $10+5+7+3 = ?$)

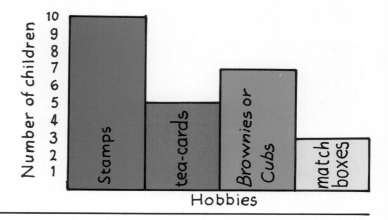

D How many sisters?

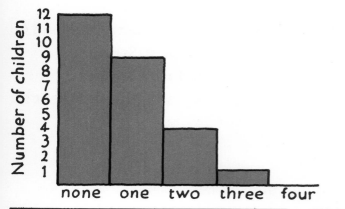

This bar chart shows you the number of sisters each child has in Sue's class. Read the chart carefully and then complete these sentences:

1 ___ of the children in Sue's class have no sisters.
2 ___ of them have one sister.
3 ___ of them have two sisters.
4 ___ of them have three sisters.
5 ___ of them has four sisters.

E How long to be born?

Hamsters grow up in four weeks. By then they are old enough to have babies themselves. They also take only two weeks to be born. They grow up faster than any other tame animal.

Here is a bar chart of the times taken for some pets to be born. From it we can read:

The hamster takes 12 days to be born.

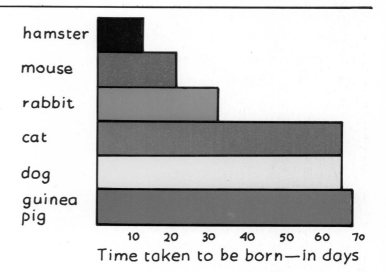

1 Write a similar sentence about each of the other five animals.
2 Which pet takes the longest time to be born?
3 Which two pets shown in the chart take the same time to be born?
4 How long does the hamster take to be born *and* grow up?

A Quick fire

Begin like this: 1 No, it isn't.

1 Is Anne's house in the High Street?
2 Is it in New Road?
3 Is the supermarket in the High Street?
4 Is the primary school in Mill Road?
5 Is Bob's house in New Road?
6 Is the post office in New Road too?

B Where questions

Begin like this: 1 It is in Mill Road.

1 Where is Nick's house?
2 Where is Anne's house?
3 Where is the post office?
4 Where is Tom's house?
5 Where is the church?
6 Where is the primary school?

C Add the right sentence

Begin like this:

1 He lives opposite Ann.

1 Bob doesn't live opposite Kate. . . .
2 Nick doesn't live in North Street. . . .
3 Tom doesn't live in New Road. . . .
4 The post office isn't in North Street. . .
5 The church isn't in New Road. . . .
6 Ann doesn't live opposite Tom. . . .

D Who, whose, which?

Begin like this:

1 Ann does.

1 Who lives opposite Bob?
2 Who lives in North Street?
3 Which big building is in Church Road?
4 Whose house is in West Street?
5 Whose house is opposite Ann's?
6 Which big building is in North Street?

E No+the right answer

Begin like this:

1 No, he lives in West Street.

1 Does Tom live in Mill Road?
2 Does Ann live in North Street?
3 Is the Rex Cinema in West Street?
4 Is Nick's house in Church Road?
5 Does Bob live opposite Kate?

F Asking questions

Ask these children where they live:

1 Bob   3 Tom   5 Kate
2 Nick   4 Ann

Begin like this:

1 YOU Where do you live, Bob?
   BOB I live in New Road.

G Who questions

The plan on the right shows you some
more houses in New Road. *Answer the
questions, like this:*

  1 Linda does.
  1 Who lives opposite Peter?
  2 Who lives opposite Ted?
  3 Who lives at No. 14?
  4 Who lives at No. 6?
  5 Who lives between Bob and Jane?
  6 Who lives between Ted and Peter?
  7 Who lives opposite Ann?
  8 Who lives next to Jane?
  9 Who lives between Jill and Bob?
  10 Who lives next to Mary?

H More questions to ask

Ask your friend where these children live:

1 Sarah   3 Jane   5 Peter
2 Dick   4 Mary   6 Jill

Begin like this:

1 YOU Where does Sarah live, Alex?
  ALEX She lives at No. 9 New Road.

I Something to do

*Copy the street plan at the top of the
opposite page. Then draw on it these
places, and name them:*

1 the library, which is between the
   post office and the Rex cinema
2 Betty's house, which is between Nick's
   house and North Street
3 Sam's house, which is opposite Kate's
4 Karen's house, which is next to Bob's,
   on the West Street side
5 the fire station, which is in West Street
   between New Road and the High
   Street; it is on the same side of the
   street as Tom's house

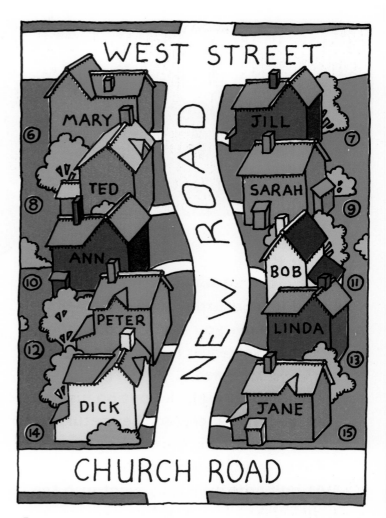

J Make a bar chart

Look back at page 21. Notice how the
bar chart was made for sisters in Sue's
class. Then make a similar bar chart for
brothers in your class. Find out how
many brothers each child has and then
make a chart to show what you find.
Write under your chart five sentences to
show what the chart tells us.

K Something to find out

*Write a sentence saying how many houses
there are in your street.*
If you live in a flat, you can write a
sentence saying how many flats there are
in the block.

STEP 12

A What Kevin did

We have pictured some of the things
Kevin did last Saturday, and we have put
in clocks to show you when he did them.
*Arrange these sentences in the same order
as the things happened:*

At half past eight he put on his new pop record.

At quarter to eleven they returned to Kevin's house and drank hot chocolate.

He called for his friend Wayne at nine o'clock.

Kevin woke up and looked at his watch. It was quarter past seven.

At half past nine they went into the heated swimming pool.

He finished breakfast at quarter to eight.

B Telling the time

At quarter past seven Kevin looked at his
watch. This is what he saw.
The long hand was pointing to 3, and the
short hand was pointing between 7 and 8.
It was quarter past seven.

 The time is
quarter past ten.

 Now it is
half past ten.

 Now it is
quarter to eleven.

 Now it is
eleven o'clock.

 Now it is
quarter past eleven.

 Now it is
half past eleven.

There are some more times
on the left. *Say where the
hands are pointing and then
what the time is. Begin like
this:*

1 *The long hand is pointing
to 3, and the short hand is
pointing between 10 and 11.
It is quarter past ten.*

C What is the time?

first · second · third

fourth · fifth · sixth

It is quarter past eight.
It is six o'clock.
It is half past nine.
It is quarter past three.
It is half past two.
It is quarter to five.

Say what time it is by each clock.
Begin like this:
1 It is half past two by the first clock.

D Ask what the time is.

Ask someone what the time is by each clock, like this:

1 YOU What is the time by the first clock, Ann?

  ANN It is quarter to four.

E A race

One Saturday Kevin called for his friend Wayne to go swimming. Wayne said he would race Kevin on his bicycle. Kevin said he would get there quicker on foot, because West Street was a one-way street, and so Wayne had to go the long way round.

They both set off at quarter to ten. The diagram shows the way Kevin ran and the way Wayne cycled. They both reached the pool on the dot of ten.

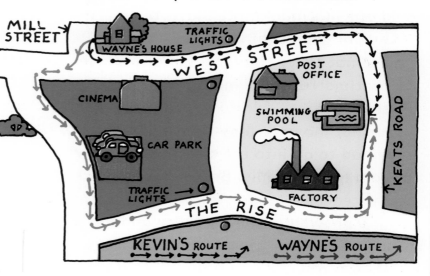

Describe the routes Kevin and Wayne took. Begin like this:
Kevin set off down Mill Street and turned left into West Street. He hurried along past the cinema, . . .
(Then describe Wayne's route in the same way.)

F Puzzle

In the race, which of the boys took longer to get from Wayne's house to the pool? Or do you think they took the same time? You might like to talk about this with your teacher.

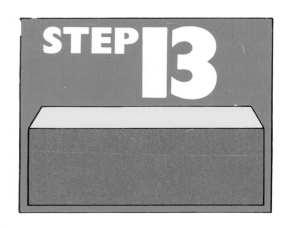

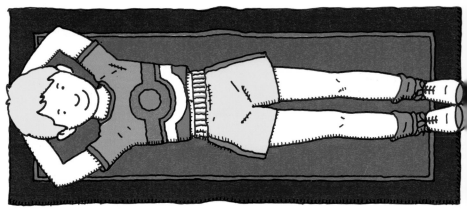

STEP 13

Tom was always boasting at school. "I'm the tallest boy in the school," he said one morning in the playground.

But Jim didn't think this was so. "I bet you're not taller than me. I'm one metre 36 centimetres tall. I measured myself," he said.

At that moment play-time ended, and they had to go into the classroom. "How tall am I, please, Miss Brown?" Tom said to the teacher.

Miss Brown gave him a ruler and he found he was one metre 34 cm tall.

"There you are," said Jim. "I told you I was taller than you."

But Tom wasn't convinced. So during the lunch hour Jim said to him: "I know! Why don't we stand back to back? Then we can easily see who is the taller."

But Tom refused to do this. He wouldn't do it because he was scared of being found in the wrong.

During P.E. Jim noticed something rather interesting.

"I'm as long as the P.E. mat," he said to himself. He ran to where Tom was idly standing and said, "I say, Tom, are you as long as the P.E. mat?"

"No, I'm not," Tom replied bluntly, "But I'm nearly as long."

"Well, that proves it!" cried Jim. "I'm taller than you because I'm as long as the mat."

At this, Tom looked crestfallen. Then he smiled. "Ah, but that's because you were lying down. It's different when you're standing up."

Jim was puzzled by Tom's reply. He went away to think about it.

A What does it mean?
Give each word or phrase its right meaning.

1 always boasting   upset
2 was not convinced   plainly; not troubling to be polite
3 idly   was left wondering
4 bluntly   did not believe
5 crestfallen   for ever praising himself
6 was puzzled   not doing anything

Begin like this:
1 always boasting:
for ever praising himself

B Answer the questions

1 Which of the boys was the boaster?
2 What was one of his boasts?
3 How tall was Jim?
4 How tall was Tom?
5 Who was the taller, Jim or Tom?
6 How much taller was Jim than Tom?
7 Did Tom believe that Jim was taller?
8 Why did Tom refuse to stand back to back?
9 Which of the boys was as long as the P.E. mat?
10 Was Tom as long as the mat?

C Think it out

1 Do you think Tom was the tallest boy?
2 Could Jim have been the tallest boy?
3 Suppose Jim was the tallest boy in the school. But Linda was taller than Jim. was Jim still the tallest boy?
4 When Jim lay down, he found he was as long as the P.E. mat. How long was the mat, then?
5 Tom said that Jim was as long as the mat only because he was lying down. Would Jim be shorter standing up?

D Write it out

Give each of these beginnings its best ending. Write out the complete sentences. Remember to begin each sentence with a capital letter and end it with a full stop.

1 A path is not as wide as   puddles.
2 A river is wider than   bushes.
3 Trees are usually taller than   fields.
4 Hills are not as high as   a stream.
5 Lakes are bigger than   mountains.
6 Lawns are not usually as big as   a road.

E Find it out

1 How tall are you?
2 Are you taller than Tom?
3 Are you as tall as Jim?
4 Cut out a strip of paper as long as Tom, and another as long as Jim. Then cut one as long as yourself. Pin the three strips on the wall. Who is the tallest—you, Tom or Jim?
5 Each of you lie on a large sheet of paper on the floor and let another pupil draw round you. Don't forget to take your shoes off. Why? Then cut out the silhouettes and put them in order—tallest to shortest.
6 Who is the tallest boy in your class?
7 Who is the tallest girl?
8 Who is the tallest pupil?
9 Are any of your pupils as tall as the teacher?

This is how you do no. 5.

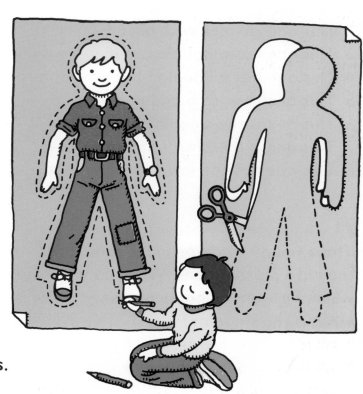

STEP 14

QUEEN STREET

Mr MORGAN

A A word puzzle

Copy this puzzle and then try to solve it with the help of the clues. The words you need are on the right.

1				
2				
3				
4				
5				
6				
7				
8				

bread	cuff
dread	stuff
letter	mice
ice	lady

1 This word rhymes with stuff.
2 This one rhymes with bread.
3 This one has a double t in it.
4 This one has a double f but no c in it.
5 This begins with b and ends with d.
6 This one is the singular of ladies.
7 This one is the plural of mouse.
8 This one has the fewest letters in it.

B Singular and plural

These nouns all name more than one: they are plural nouns. What do we write when we want to name one only? That is, what is the singular?

1 mice	4 boxes	7 children
2 babies	5 matches	8 geese
3 teeth	6 stories	9 policemen

Mr Smith lives next door to Mr Morgan in Queen Street. Mrs James lives between Mr Smith and Mrs Lee. Mr Taylor's house is opposite Mr Morgan's. Mr Davies is Mr Taylor's neighbour. The man who lives opposite Mrs Lee is called Mr Roberts. Mrs Squeers lives between Mr Roberts and Mr Davies.
Draw your own map of Queen Street and write the names of the people on their houses.

D Words into sentences

Make six complete sentences by adding the right verb to each noun. Remember to start each sentence with a capital letter and end it with a full stop.

	NOUN	VERB
1	Operations	are flown.
2	Race-horses	is baked.
3	Aeroplanes	are painted.
4	Books	are performed.
5	Bread	are ridden.
6	Pictures	are written.

E By whom

Write by whom the actions are done.
Begin like this:
1 Operations are performed by surgeons.

28

F Rhymes

There was a young fellow in Crete
Who stood on his head in the street.
    Said he, 'It is clear
    If I mean to stay here
I shall have to shake hands with my feet.'

Limericks would not be such fun if the lines didn't rhyme. Which words rhyme with which?

Notice that rhymes don't always have the same spelling. It is the sound rather than the spelling that matters.
Clear rhymes with here, though their spellings are quite different.
Now try to pair each of these words with the word it rhymes with. Do one column at a time.

1	pair	crack	6 bricks	word
2	black	round	7 meat	there
3	found	door	8 teach	six
4	blue	hair	9 third	feet
5	four	chew	10 chair	reach

G A rhyme puzzle

Can you find the rhyme words from these clues? The first answer is money.

1 You can spend it and it rhymes with *honey*.
2 It is the name of a month and it rhymes with *moon*.
3 You climb it and it rhymes with *Jill*.
4 It's a boy's name rhyming with *sack*.
5 It's a girls' name rhyming with *man*.
6 It's a piece of crockery and it rhymes with *eight*.
7 It runs and rhymes with *cream*.

H Mystery message

Copy the picture of the ruler. Then read the letters in the coloured patch. Write each letter above its correct mark on the ruler. For example, the letter C goes above the number 4 on the ruler. The letter O goes above six different numbers. When you have written all the letters above the ruler, they should spell a message.

O 1 2 3 4 5 6 7 8 9 10 11 12 13 14 15 16 17 18

C 4	N 0	O 1, 6, 7, 11, 13, 16
H 5	S 3	R 14, 15
L 8	T 10	
M 12	W 17	

I Sleeping times

Make a bar chart of how long pets sleep for. Choose five or six pets from among those kept by your friends or classmates. You may have to guess at some of the sleeping times. Put in your own sleeping time as well. (See page 31 D.)

J Your pet

Write about your pet. If you haven't got one, write about the one you would like to have.
You could write:
where to keep him;
what he eats;
where he sleeps;
how cuddly he is;
how he moves and plays;
what noises he makes;
whether he calls to you;
how often you clean his cage.

STEP 15

PENNY Gary, why do you wake so early? It's only half past seven.

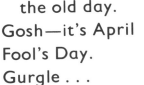

PENNY I must tear off the old day. Gosh—it's April Fool's Day.

BABY Gurgle . . .

PENNY This'll fool Mum. I'll turn the clock on 1 hour.

MUM Help! Look at the time, Penny. You'll be late for school.

PENNY It's all right, Mum. Miss Lee said I could be late today.

MUM I'm sure she didn't . . . Now I've burnt the toast, and look at Gary . . . It's quarter past nine!

PENNY April Fool, Mum! It's only quarter past eight.

A I-spy

How many of these things
can you see in the pictures?
Make a list. There should be a dozen.

football	plate	breakfast food
teddy-bear	telephone	dish
chair	cat	star
calendar	chest	dog
rainbow	camera	spoon
rattle	toast	table
clock	cot	bottle

B Quiz

1 What is the baby called?
2 What is Penny doing in the second
   picture?
3 What is she doing in the next picture?
4 Who woke Penny up?
5 What was the date when Penny played
   her April Fool joke?
6 What was her April Fool joke?
7 What did the baby do with his food?
8 Why did Penny's mum get in a flap?
9 What was the *real* time when Penny's
   mum said, "You'll be late for school?"
10 How long a time actually passed
   between what happened in the first
   picture and in the last picture?

C Give the time

*Put in the times when you think they were
most likely to do these things:*
1 Penny gave the baby his bottle at . . .
2 Gary had tea at . . .
3 Penny played hopscotch during
   lunch time at . . .
4 Penny played chess with her dad at . . .

D Puzzle time

*Draw a clock face
to help you solve
these puzzles:*

1 Sandra's dog sleeps from 10 o'clock
   at night till 7 o'clock in the morning.
   How long does he sleep?
2 Bob's cat sleeps two hours in the
   morning; she has a cat-nap for a
   couple of hours in the afternoon, and
   she usually sleeps from midnight to
   6 o'clock in the morning. How long
   does she usually sleep?
3 Stephen's hamster sleeps all day. He
   sleeps from 7 o'clock in the morning
   till 7 o'clock in the evening, when he
   wakes up to eat and play. Then he
   stays awake all night till 7 o'clock next
   morning. How long does he sleep?

E How much later?

Say how many minutes later it is now.
Begin like this:
1 It is five minutes later now.

F Write a story

Write the story of the pictures on page 30.
This is how Colin started:
On 1st April the baby woke Penny up
early. It was only half past seven . . .

STEP 16

	Country
AUS	Australia
CDN	Canada
D	Germany
DK	Denmark
F	France
GB	Great Britain
GR	Greece
I	Italy
IND	India
IS	Iceland

A Add the right sentence

1 D doesn't stand for Denmark. It stands for Germany.
1 D doesn't stand for Denmark.
2 CDN doesn't stand for China.
3 The red car doesn't come from Italy.
4 The third car doesn't come from India.
5 The first car doesn't come from Spain.
6 GR doesn't stand for Great Britain.

B Answer these questions

1 Where does the second car come from?
2 Where does the blue car come from?
3 What does GB stand for?
4 Does D stand for Denmark or Germany?
5 Does the red car come from Denmark?
6 What colour is the car from France?

C Ask someone these questions

1 YOU Where does the fourth car come from, Ann?

ANN It comes from Canada.

1 Ask where the fourth car comes from.
2 Ask where the red car comes from.
3 Ask where the third car comes from.
4 Ask where the one with D comes from.
5 Ask what DK stands for.

D Draw and write

Here are three more cars. *Draw them and then write three sentences, one to say where each car comes from.*

E Prepared dictation

The first car driven by a petrol engine was sold in 1885. It was made by Karl Benz in Germany. Henry Ford produced his first car in 1892. The first Rolls Royce appeared in 1904. It had the same shape radiator as it has today.

BEFORE   CRASH   AFTER

G Scatty!

1 How many drinks did Scatty spill?
2 How many has he still got?

F Plus and minus

The signs +, called 'plus', and —, called 'minus', were invented in the 1400s. Merchants first used the signs when they weighed bales of wool. If the bale weighed more than the right weight, they marked it +. 'Plus' is Latin for 'more'. If the bale weighed less than the right weight, they marked it —. 'Minus' is Latin for 'less'. We use the same signs today in our sums.

For example, 2 and 3 more is written $2+3$. We also use another sign =, which means 'equals'. So we might write: $2+3 = 5$ as a quick way of saying 2 and 3 more equals 5 all together. In the same way, $3-2 = 1$ is a quick way of saying 3 and 2 less equals 1.

1 Write these as sentences with words:
  a $3+2 = 5$ b $5-3 = 2$
  c $5-2 = 3$ d $5-5 = 0$
2 Did you notice the special number sign 0? It is called 'zero' and means nothing. Write another number sentence like 1 (d) and put it in words as well.

3 The Indians invented zero in 600 A.D.
  a Was zero invented before + and —?
  b How long ago was zero invented?

H Make a sum

Look at the pictures of Scatty again. In the first picture he has three drinks on one tray and two more on another.
1 Make up a sum about the first picture, with + and = in it.
2 Make up a sum about the second with — and = in it.

I A poem to illustrate
by *Dorothy W. Baruch*

Automobiles
          in
          a
          row
Wait to go
While the signal says:
                    STOP

Bells ring
Ting-a-ling
Red light gone!
Green light's on!
Horns blow!
And the row
          starts
            to GO.

1 Write out the poem, using coloured letters for some of the words in it.
2 Draw a coloured picture to go with the poem.

STEP 17

TED   KATE   SARAH

CHARLES   BOB

A Right or left?

All five children have just put up their hands. Some have put up their right hands and some their left. *Can you put the missing word in each sentence? Begin like this:*

1 Sarah has just put up her right hand.

1 Sarah has just put up her ___ hand.
2 Ted has just put up his ___ hand.
3 Charles and Kate have just put up their ___ hands.
4 Bob has just put up his ___ hand.
5 Kate and Sarah have just put up their ___ hands.

B Asking questions

Ask the children which hands they have put up. Begin like this:

1 YOU Which hand have you put up, Ted?
   TED   I have put up my left hand.

C Writing sentences

Write five sentences to say which hand each child is holding up in the picture. Begin like this:
1 Ted is holding up his left hand.

D Mixed questions

1 Which hand is Kate holding up?
2 Which boy is holding up his right hand?
3 Is Sarah holding up her left hand?
4 Is Bob holding up his right hand or his left?
5 How many of the children are holding up their right hands?
6 How many of the boys are holding up their left hands?

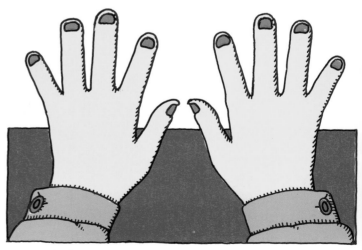

left hand   right hand

TOM LUCY CHARLES TRACEY JAMES

E O'Grady

These children are playing O'Grady.
The leader has just said "O'Grady says
hold up your left leg."
Lucy is holding up her right leg, so she
is wrong. Who else is wrong?

F The children speaking

They all know their mistakes now, and
can say which leg they are standing on.
What does each child say? Begin like this:
1 TOM I am standing on my right leg.

H Mirror images

1 The right hand looks almost exactly
the same as its image in the mirror.
Can you say how the right hand and
its reflection are different?
2 Take a small sheet of paper. Fold it,
then smooth it flat. Drop a blob of ink
on the crease; paint will do as well.
Now fold the paper again and press
it tight. Open the fold once more and
you may see a pattern like this.
What do you notice about the pattern?
Write two or three sentences to say
what it reminds you of.

G Ask these questions

Begin like this:
YOU How many of the children are
standing on their right legs, Ann?
ANN Three are.

Ask someone:
1 how many of the children are standing
on their right legs;
2 how many of the boys are standing on
their right legs;
3 how many of the children are holding
up their left legs;
4 which girl is standing on her left leg;
5 which boy is holding up his right leg;
6 which leg Charles is holding up.

STEP 18

There was once a little boy whose real name was George, but everyone called him Tiny. He was only four years old, so you could not expect him to be very big. Still, he was rather small even for four. Some people said he was only three, but Tiny did not like people who said that.

Tiny had two sisters, Judy and May. Judy was ten and May was eight, and of course they both went to school.

People said to Tiny: "How nice for you to have two big sisters to look after you and play with you."

Sometimes Tiny did think it was nice. But sometimes he thought it was horrid. When Judy and May read to him or played hide-and-seek with him, he thought it was nice to have two sisters. But when they said: "Go away, you're too little to understand!" then he thought it was horrid to have any sisters at all. And when they whispered secrets to each other and would not let him hear, he cried with rage.

Judy had a white rabbit for a pet, and May had a pair of golden hamsters. The girls fed them and cleaned out their cages all by themselves.

Tiny wanted a pet as well. His mother promised him that he should have one when he was old enough to look after it properly himself. But Tiny wanted one now, this very minute.

One day Judy and May were playing telegrams. One of them wrote a few words on a slip of yellow paper and then put it in an orange envelope. They dressed Tiny up as the telegram boy. He had to ring the front door bell and bang with the knocker as well. Then he handed the telegram to whichever of the girls came to the door.

Tiny liked ringing the bell and banging the knocker. But he wanted the girls to read the telegram aloud to him, because he couldn't read. They wouldn't do this.

"You spoil the game," they said crossly. "Telegram boys never ask to hear what is in the telegram. Don't be silly!"

"Then I won't play," said Tiny, and he stamped his feet and ran off on his own.

A Questions

1 Why was George called Tiny?
2 How much older was May than Tiny?
3 Who was the oldest of the three children?
4 Two things made Tiny think it nice to have two sisters. What were they?
5 What two things made Tiny dislike his sisters?
6 When was his mother going to let Tiny keep a pet of his own?
7 What made Tiny stamp his feet and run off on his own?
8 The knocker *banged*. What other noises are made in the story?

B Noisy sentences

*Make short but complete sentences by giving
each beginning its best ending, like this:*

1 Knockers bang.

1 Knockers	bark.
2 Clocks	hiss.
3 Chains	bleat.
4 Dogs	bang.
5 Cats	pop.
6 Sheep	purr.
7 Balloons	crack.
8 Whips	tick.
9 Rusty hinges	clank.
10 Boiling kettles	creak.

C Asking questions

Ask someone what noise each of these makes.

1 a bee   3 a mouse   5 a whip
2 a pig   4 steam   6 a frog

Begin like this:

1 YOU   What noise does a bee make, Ali?
   ALI   It buzzes.

D More sounds

Can you complete these?

1 the rustling of leaves in the breeze
2 the clatter of horses hoofs
3 the wail of a siren
4 the __ of car brakes
5 the __ of the wind
6 the __ of little feet
7 the __ of a rotary saw
8 the __ of a small bell
9 the __ of dishes in the kitchen sink
10 the __ of a tap in need of a washer

E Something to find out

What noises do these make?

1 donkeys   3 horses   5 cockerels
2 bulls   4 wolves   6 elephants

F Something to learn by heart

Every Thursday morning,
Before you're quite awake,
Without the slightest warning
The house begins to shake
    With a Biff! Bang!
    Biff! Bang! Bash!

It's the Dustman who begins
    (Bang! Crash!)
To empty both the bins
Of their rubbish and their ash,
    With a Biff! Bang!
    Biff! Bang! Bash!

           Clive Sansom

STEP 19

a week ago **3 weeks ago** **last Saturday**
a fortnight ago **last Friday**

| JANUARY | | | | | | |
Sun	Mon	Tues	Wed	Thur	Fri	Sat
—	—	1	2	3	4	5
6	(7)	8	9	10	11	12
13	(14)	15	16	17	18	19
20	(21)	22	23	24	(25)	(26)
(27)	(28)	(29)	(30)	(31)	—	—

yesterday today tomorrow
the day before yesterday **the day after tomorrow**

A The calendar

Let us pretend that it is now January.
The month began on a Tuesday.
It is 29th January today. It was 28th
January yesterday. It will be 30th
January tomorrow.
*By looking at the calendar, answer the
questions below. Begin like this:*
1 It was a Tuesday.

1 What day was 1st January?
2 What day was 22nd January?
3 What day was 18th January?
4 What day was 23rd January?
5 What day is it today?
6 What day will 31st January be?

B Dates

Begin like this: 1 It was 23rd January.

1 What was the date last Wednesday?
2 What was the date yesterday?
3 What was the date a week ago?
4 What was the date last Friday?
5 What is the date today?
6 What will the date be tomorrow?
7 What will it be the day after tomorrow?
8 What was the date last Saturday?

C How many days?

*Read the rhyme and then answer the
questions below. Begin like this:*
1 There are thirty-one.
Thirty days hath September,
April, June and November.
All the rest have thirty-one
Excepting February alone,
Which has but twenty-eight days clear
And twenty-nine in each leap year.

1 How many days are there in August?
2 How many are there in November?
3 How many are there in January?
4 Are there thirty or thirty-one in June?
5 Are there thirty days in April?
6 Are there thirty in July?
7 How many are there usually in
February?
7 When are there twenty-nine days in
February?

D Days of the week

Here are the days of the week. *Put them
in their right order, beginning with Sunday.*
Tuesday   Friday   Thursday
Saturday   Sunday   Monday   Wednesday

38

E Putting the months in order

tenth	March
fourth	August
first	December
twelfth	June
second	October
sixth	January
third	May
ninth	July
fifth	November
eighth	February
seventh	September
eleventh	April

Make twelve sentences to say what the first, second, third . . . month is. Check your spelling with the lists above. Begin like this:

1 The first month is January.
2 The second month is . . .

F Let's pretend

To answer these questions we have to use pretend dates. *Begin like this:*

1 It was 22nd June 1974.

1 If it is 23rd June 1974 today, what was it yesterday?
2 If it is 2nd August 1973 today, what will it be tomorrow?
3 If it is 17th October 1974 today, what was it the day before yesterday?
4 If it was 21st December 1975 yesterday, what is it today?
5 If it will be 3rd January 1978 tomorrow, what is it today?
6 If it was 12th February 1974 yesterday, what will it be tomorrow?

G Real dates

Write down the date of:
1 your next birthday   2 next Christmas
3 last New Year's day   4 today
5 yesterday   6 tomorrow
7 the day on which you were born
8 the day before yesterday

H Birthdays

has a birthday in

A SET OF CHILDREN   A SET OF MONTHS

This is called a mapping. Each arrow stands for the words 'has a birthday in'.

1 In what month does Gary's birthday come?
2 In what month is Fred's birthday?
3 Is Ian's birthday in March or April?
4 What is Ted's birthday?
5 When do both Ted and Pam have their birthdays?
6 In what month does no one have a birthday?

Write down the names of the children in your group and map their birthdays.

A A street map

Look at the map. It shows part of Lower Road. Wayne lives opposite Jane. He also lives next to Ann. So Wayne is Ann's neighbour. Ann lives between Kevin and Wayne. So Kevin is Ann's neighbour on one side, and Wayne is her neighbour on the other side.

There is a name missing. *Can you put it in?*

1 Ann lives opposite __.
2 Tom lives next to __.
3 Peter lives between Jane and __.
4 __ lives opposite Tom.
5 Jane lives next to __.
6 __ lives next to Ann.
7 Tom's neighbour is __.
8 Jane's neighbour is __.
9 Peter's neighbour on one side is a girl called __.
10 His neighbour on the other side is __.

B Writing sentences

1 Pretend you are Kevin. Write two sentences to say who lives opposite you and who lives on each side of you.
2 Pretend you are Wendy. Write two sentences to say who lives opposite you and who your neighbours are.

C Asking questions

Begin like this:

1 YOU Who lives next to Carole, Tom?
  TOM Kevin does.

Ask someone, who lives

1 next to Carole
2 opposite Peter
3 next to Wayne
4 between Carole and Ann
5 opposite Kevin
6 next to Tom

D A puzzle

Eight children are playing a game. Four are standing on one side of a rope and four on the other side. Bob is standing opposite Alec. Linda's only neighbour is Alec. Sue is standing opposite Linda and next to Bob. Liz is standing between Ted and Alec. Stephen is opposite Ted, and Karen is between Stephen and Bob.

Copy the diagram, and put in all the names.

E Where do they live?

The children in each of these groups all live in the same street. By using the table you can find out where they must live. *Make sentences to say where they live, and make sure you separate the names with commas.*

1 Bob, Tony, Mary and Ruth
2 Stephen, Mike, Susan and Margaret
3 Elizabeth, Ron, Bill and Alec
4 Ted, Karen, Dick, Helen and Kevin
5 Linda, George, Simon, Derek and Jean

Name	Street
Alec	George Street
Linda	Gravel Hill
Kevin	Lower Road
Tony	Bluebell Crescent
Susan	Bridge Street

Begin like this:

1 Bob, Tony, Mary and Ruth all live in Bluebell Crescent.

F Villages

This is a map of Marbury and the nearby villages.
It shows which villages have a post office, a garage, a supermarket, a church, and so on.
Write a sentence like this about all the other villages on the map.
Marbury has a Post Office, a garage and a church, but no supermarket.

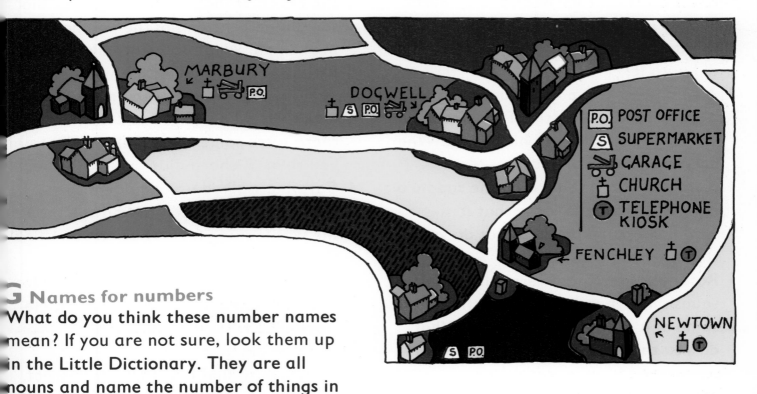

G Names for numbers

What do you think these number names mean? If you are not sure, look them up in the Little Dictionary. They are all nouns and name the number of things in a group.

1 dozen   3 score   5 trio
2 century   4 four score 6 quartet

H To find out

Why do you think we count in tens?
(Hint: do you ever count on your fingers?)

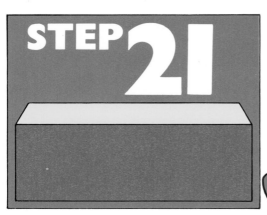

STEP 21

A What did they do?

Linda answered these questions very sensibly. You will find her answers at the end. *Which was her answer to each question?*

1 Tom was running across the playground. Suddenly he saw a small boy right in front of him. He didn't knock him over. What do you think he did?

2 Wendy found 10p in the playground. It was not hers. What do you think she did with it?

3 A small boy at a picnic was trying to get the top off a bottle of coca-cola. He was tugging at it with his fingers. What do you think Kevin did?

4 Kate was three years old. The saddle of her tricycle was so loose that it wobbled up and down. What do you think her big brother did?

5 Rose was carrying a very full glass of squash. Her hand shook and she spilt some of it on the kitchen floor. What do you think she did?

He tightened it up with a spanner.
He took it off with a bottle opener.
She wiped it up with the floor cloth.
She took it to the teacher.
He swerved and missed him.

B What do you think?

Now you say what you think they did.

1 There was a nail sticking out of the piece of wood. John wanted to use the piece as a bat. What do you think he did?

2 Susan hit her foot against a pebble on the beach. It jagged the nail of her big toe and left the end of the nail half broken off. What do you think she did?

3 Richard saw a man with a white stick standing at the side of the road. It looked as if he wanted to cross, but there were some cars coming. What do you think Richard did?

4 Caroline walked up and down the street, but she could not find the shop she was looking for. What do you think she did?

5 Colin was reading a book about ponies and came across the word *crupper*. He wondered what it meant. What do you think he did?

6 Dave had to find No. 16 Bridge Street, to deliver a parcel to Mrs Tapp. He found No. 15, but the next house had lost its number. What do you think he did?

C What with?

They did these things yesterday. *Say what they did them with, by giving each beginning its best ending.*

BEGINNINGS

1 Mr Carter dug his garden
2 Caroline cut out a picture
3 Ted cut his birthday cake
4 Mrs Banks swept her carpet
5 Christopher smoothed the wood
6 Anna beat the eggs

ENDINGS

with a big knife.
with a whisk.
with sandpaper.
with scissors.
with a spade.
with a brush.

 Ted Mr Carter  Anna  Christopher  Caroline  Mrs Banks

D What were the questions?

On the right are the answers to six questions about the sentences in C. *What questions were they the answers to? Begin like this:*

1 What did Mr Carter dig his garden with?

   He dug it with a spade.

1 He dug it with a spade.
2 She cut it out with scissors.
3 He cut it with a big knife.
4 Mrs Banks did.
5 Yes, he did.
6 No, she beat them with a whisk.

E House numbers

On page 23 there is a street map of New Road. The houses in New Road are numbered in a special way. But the first five houses are not shown. *Draw a map of the road and show on which side Numbers 1, 2, 3, 4 and 5 are.*

F Questions about New Road

1 Have the houses on Jill's side of the road got odd or even numbers?
2 What sort of numbers have the houses on the other side of the road?
3 How many houses have odd numbers?
4 Has Peter's house got an odd number?
5 How many houses are there on the same side as No. 10?

G My street

Write about your street. You could say what sort of houses there are, how they are numbered, who lives in them, what goes on in the street . . .

STEP 22

A Word changing

This word game can be good fun. It also makes you think quickly and helps to improve your spelling.

The first player chooses any four-letter word that contains two vowel letters (A E I O U) He might, for example, choose the word DARE.

The second player then has to change one letter to make a new word. Only ten seconds are allowed. Perhaps he chooses DART.

The next player has again to change a single letter to make yet another new word. Perhaps he changes the D for a P and makes the word PART.

Each player in turn has to make a new word by changing one letter only. But he can't use a word if it has already been used. The game might go on like this:

PORT → SORT → SORE → MORE → MARE → CARE → BARE → BORE → . . .

Any player who fails to make a new word in ten seconds drops out, till only one player—the winner—is left.

Names of people, places, and special goods like Ajax, Dane—any words that begin with a capital letter—are not allowed.

Now see if you can answer these questions about the game.

1 Which of these words could be used by the first player?
   RARE MUST EAR MOON FLOOR
2 How many letters can the second player change?
3 How long is each player given to think of a new word?
4 Which of these words are not allowed? Jill, fond, York, Peru, foot, Webb.
5 How many of the words in brackets could you choose to continue this list?
   COAL, COAT GOAT (GOOD, GOAL, BOAT, GOAD, COAT, COST, GOLD, MOAT, FOAL.)
6 Which words could you choose to continue the game that had got to BORE?
   CORE, BOOT, SORE, HARE, BORN

B Why?

The answer to the first question below is: Because there is only one vowel in it. It is really a short form of a longer answer: (He can't begin with PART) because there is only one vowel in it.
Now answer all the questions and begin each answer with Because . . .

1 Why can't the first player begin with the word PART?
2 Why can't a player give the word PERU as his new word?
3 The last word was DEAR. Why can't Kevin make DOOR his new word?
4 Why can't the first player start with the word WEIGH?
5 Why can't Linda change BEAT into MEAT in a game which has gone like this?
   MEAT, MEAL, REAL, SEAL, SEAT, HEAT, BEAT. . .

C Because

Make up a sentence in which you need each of the reasons given in the list. You could begin like this:

1 The little boy is crying because he has cut himself.

1 because he has cut himself.
2 because she is too hot.
3 because they saw a policeman coming.
4 because she has just heard a funny story.
5 because it is raining hard.
6 because he wants to reach the roof.

D To make you think

Why do these pictures look silly? Someone is in the wrong place. In which picture ought that person to be? Write three sentences about each picture. This is what Shirley wrote for the first one.

1 *This picture looks silly because guitarists don't stand in rivers like that. Only fishermen do that. The guitarist ought to be in the picture of the dance.*

E Use your imagination

Take another look at the pictures. They look silly. But are you sure things couldn't have happened like that? Could there have been some very special reason? Try to think of a possible reason for what is happening in each picture and explain to the group how it happened, or write a story explaining how it happened. There is a clue to one in the picture on the right.

F A game to play

Collect a trayful of things like those shown in the picture. Heap together a small set of the things, for a definite reason. It might be because they are the same colour, or all have flat sides. The other players, in turn, have to say why you have put them together. The first player to guess your reason makes the next set. And so on.

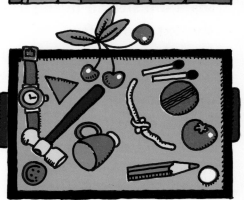

STEP 23

A Where are they?

There is a diagram of the classroom on the blackboard, and Wayne is standing at the blackboard with his back to the class. The children have changed places, so he doesn't know where they are sitting. He has to ask one of them where he is sitting, and then he has to try to find his position on the diagram and write in the name.

WAYNE Where are you sitting now, Steve?

STEVE   I am sitting in the middle row and there is only one seat on my right.

Wayne has found the right seat and written in Steve's name.

Where would Wayne have written their names if he had been given these replies?

1 SUE I am sitting in the second row and there are two seats on my left and two on my right.

2 BOB I am sitting in the fourth row on the extreme left.

3 GARY I am sitting on Steve's right.

4 WENDY I am sitting in the row in front of Steve, and my seat is against the wall on the right.

5 ALAN I am one from the left in the back row.

6 CAROLE I am right in the middle.

B Your classroom

Make a similar diagram of your own classroom. Write your name where you are sitting. Then write the name of the nearest boy or girl whose first name begins with C, D, E, or F.

Under the diagram, write sentences to say where you are sitting and where the other pupil is sitting.

C No, no, Scatty

KEVIN   Hullo, Scatty!

SCATTY Hello! Hello!
I'm Scatty, I'm Scatty.
I'm not Ted. I'm not Nick . . .

KEVIN   Yes, I know, I know, but listen;
What are 2 and 8, Scatty?

SCATTY 2 and 8 are twenty-eight.

KEVIN   No, no, Scatty. What are 2 plus 8?

SCATTY But why didn't you say so?
2 plus 8 equals 10.

D Number puzzles

The biggest number you can make out of the digits (figures) 1, 6 and 2 is 621. The smallest number is 126. What is the biggest number your can make out of the digits 3 and 7? What is the smallest number you can make out of them? What is the biggest number you can make out of the digits 4, 2 and 8? What is the smallest number?

3 Think of an even number. Any number will do. Now add 1 on to it. What sort of number do you get, odd or even?

4 Think of two odd numbers. Any ones will do, and they don't have to be the same. Add them together. What sort of number do you get, odd or even? Is this always so, no matter what odd numbers you begin with?

E Time passes

Ann made this clock face. It shows what she is going to do on Wednesday. It also shows, roughly, the time she will spend on each thing she plans to do. For example, she will spend quite a lot of time painting and writing English, but not very much time in drinking milk. Ann's diagram is called a pie chart.

Pretend it is the middle of Wednesday morning. Ann has cut off the parts of her pie chart for things she has already done.

1 Write a sentence to say what she has already done.

2 Say what she is doing now. (Look at the clock hand.)

3 Say what she is just going to do.

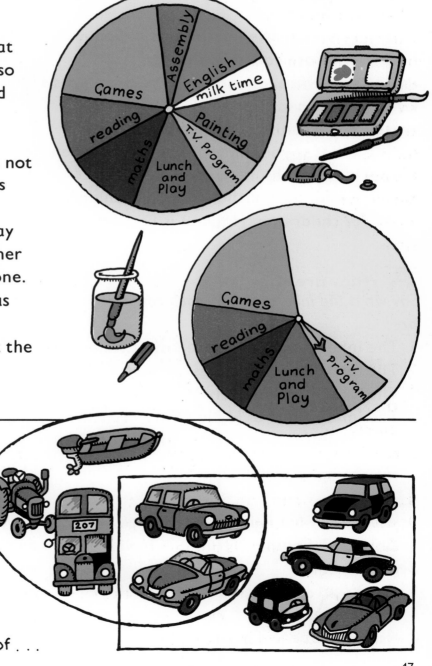

F Sets

There are three sets of things in the picture—a set of green things, a set of cars and a set of green cars. Write three sentences to say where the sets are. Begin like this:

Where the egg shape and the oblong shape overlap, I can see a set of . . .

47

STEP 24

MR LEE	What is this country, Kathy?
KATHY	It's Spain.
MR LEE	What are the inhabitants of Spain called, Mark?
MARK	They are called Spaniards.
MR LEE	And what language do the Spaniards speak, Karen?
KAREN	They speak Spanish.
MR LEE	Yes, Spanish is their mother tongue.
	What is your mother tongue, Stephen?
STEPHEN	It's English.
MR LEE	Good, our mother tongue is English, and the mother tongue of children in Holland is Dutch.

A What are they?

Say what the inhabitants of each country are:

1 The inhabitants of France   are Chinese.
2 The inhabitants of Wales   are Italian.
3 The inhabitants of Italy   are Welsh.
4 The inhabitants of Holland are French.
5 The inhabitants of China   are Dutch.

B Ask

Ask someone what language they speak in:
1 China   2 Spain   3 Italy   4 Holland
Begin like this:

1 YOU   What language do they speak in China, Tom?

  TOM   They speak Chinese.

C Brief conversations

Name	Country	Mother tongue
Marcelle	France	French
John	Australia	English
Pedro	Spain	Spanish
Anneke	Holland	Dutch
Olaf	Denmark	Danish

Ask the children where they come from and then what language they speak, like this:

YOU **Where do you come from Marcelle?**

MARCELLE   I come from France.

YOU **What language do you speak?**

MARCELLE   I speak French.

D More conversations

Make conversations about the pictures.
By choosing the right parts from the frame
you can begin in nine different ways.
Here is one way:

ALLY Which picture are you looking at, Bob?
BOB   I'm looking at the picture of the clown.
ALLY What is he doing?
      My eyes are bad today.
BOB   He is standing on a horse's back.

Which person	are you talking about, Bob?
Which picture	are you looking at, Bob?
Which one	are you pointing to, Bob?

I am talking about	the nurse.
I'm looking at	the goalkeeper.
I'm pointing to	the picture of the clown.
	the picture of the girl.

What is he doing?	I can't see very well.
	My glasses are broken.
What is she doing?	The picture is torn.
	My eyes are bad today.

He is	leaping into the air.
	standing on a horse's back.
She is	giving her patient a drink.
	eating a huge ice cream.

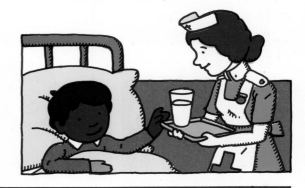

E Distances

Look at the street map on page 22. It is 50 metres from the cinema to the post office. About how far is it from Kate's house to Nick's house?

49

STEP 25

KAREN

COLIN

PETER

LIZ

LINDA

STEVE

A Who has just . . . ?

Begin like this: 1 Linda has.

1 Who has just climbed up some steps?
2 Who has just picked some flowers?
3 Who has just fallen off her bicycle?
4 Who has just saved a goal?
5 Who has just bought a new record?
6 Who has just made a model plane?

B Who is going to . . . ?

Begin like this: 1 Liz is.

1 Who is going to put some flowers in a vase in a moment?
2 Who is going to dive in a moment?
3 Who is going to play a record?
4 Who is going to launch his plane?
5 Who is going to pick herself up in a moment?
6 Who is going to take a goal kick?

C Adding sentences

The sentences below tell you what the children are doing in the pictures. *Add one sentence in front of each to say what the child has just done. Add another after, to say what he or she is going to do in a moment.* Begin like this:

1 Karen has just fallen off her bicycle.
   She is lying on the ground now.
   In a moment she is going to pick herself up.

1 Karen is lying on the ground now.
2 Colin has the plane in his hand now.
3 Peter is putting the record on now.
4 Liz is smelling the flowers now.
5 Linda is standing on the top board now.
6 Steve is holding the ball now.

D Short forms

Steve is the short form of Stephen, and Babs is the short form of Barbara. *Can you pair each of these short names with its full name?*

Short name	Full name
1 Sam	Thomas
2 Chris	Catherine
3 Tom	Henry
4 Sue	Elizabeth
5 Hal	Samuel
6 Kate	Susan
7 Dick	Rebecca
8 Liz	Edward
9 Ted	Christine
10 Becky	Richard

E Nursery rhymes

How well do you remember your nursery rhymes? Here are some names from the rhymes? *Use them to answer the questions.*

Simple Simon Mary
Old King Cole Polly Flinders
Humpty Dumpty Jack Sprat
Jack Horner Sukey
Old Mother Hubbard Tom

1 Who sat in a corner?
2 Who had a little lamb?
3 Who took the kettle off?
4 Who had a great fall?
5 Who stole a pig and ran away?
6 Who called for his pipe?
7 Who couldn't eat any fat?
8 Who went a-fishing?
9 Who sat among the cinders?
10 Who went to the baker's to buy her dog some bread?

F What next?

Write some sentences about each of these pictures. Make up a story if you can. Say what is happening now, and what is going to happen.

51

STEP 26

Look, Tom, here's a hose-pipe.

Good, now we can have some fun. Turn on the tap, Kate.

O.K. I've turned it on.

Ouch! Stop it, Tom. You're soaking me.

Oh, dear, nothing is coming out.

Is there any dirt in the nozzle, Tom? Will you have a look?

O.K. I'm looking.

Ouch! Stop it, Kate. Turn off the tap. You're soaking me.

A Questions

1 Who found the hose-pipe?
2 Who said, "Good, now we can have some fun"?
3 Did Tom or Kate pick up the end of the hose-pipe?
4 Which of them turned on the tap?
5 What did Tom do when the water came on?
6 Who is speaking in the fourth picture?
7 Why did Tom look into the nozzle?
8 What happened while he was looking?

B Prick the bubbles

In strip pictures, what the people say is often written in bubbles. Can you write out the bubbles as the words would be written in a play-book? You did some in Step 24.
Begin like this:

KATE Look, Tom, here's a hose-pipe.

TOM Good, now we can have some fun . . .

C Sets

Draw a set of people for each pair of sentences below. Write the sentences under your drawings.

1 There are some blue people in this set. There are no fat people here.
2 There are some thin people in this set. There are no blue people here.
3 There are some short people here. There are some blue people.
   (Hint: there may be tall, red people as well.)

52

D What is it?

In this picture strip you can find several clues to what is inside the box.
Can you work out what it might be? Say what you think it is, and give your reasons.

E Make a picture strip

Draw a picture strip and write bubbles to show what people are saying for this conversation:

SIMON I say, it's been raining.

SUE How do you know?

SIMON Look at the lawn.

SUE Oh, yes, it's dripping wet. But it might not have been raining.

SIMON No, not a cloud.

SUE Ah, I know what probably happened. Look at that hose.

SIMON Yes, somebody's been hosing the lawn.

SUE Scatty, I expect!

F Continue the story

Can you continue this in conversation form to make a complete story?

MOTHER The breakfast is ready.

FATHER The children are not down yet, dear.

MOTHER I wonder what they are doing. They will be late for school.

FATHER I will call them. Kevin! Liz!

MOTHER Not a sound. You start your breakfast, dear, and I will go and see what is going on.

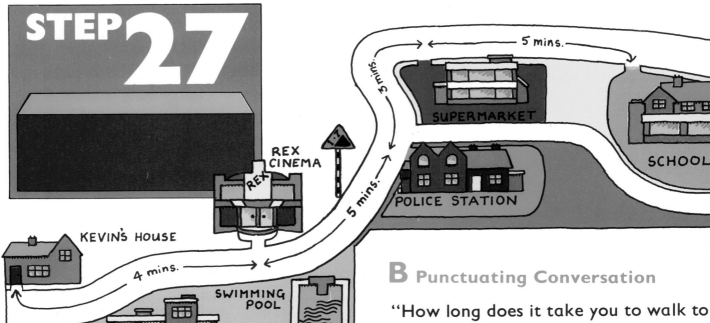

STEP 27

A How long does it take?

Kevin walks to school every morning. It takes him four minutes to reach the cinema. It takes him another five minutes to get to the Police Station. So, from his house to the Police Station takes him nine minutes.

Now try to answer the questions below. Begin like this: 1 It takes him three minutes.

1 How long does it take Kevin to walk from the Police Station to the Supermarket?
2 How long does it take him to get to school from the Supermarket?
3 How long does Kevin's walk from the cinema to the Police Station take him?
4 How long does it take him to go from the cinema to the Supermarket?
5 How long does it take him to walk from the Police Station to School?
6 How long does the whole journey from home to school take Kevin?

B Punctuating Conversation

"How long does it take you to walk to school, Kevin?" asked Linda.
"It takes me seventeen minutes if I don't stop on the way," replied Kevin.
Notice very carefully how Linda's question is set out and then how Kevin's reply is set out. This is how conversation is set out in stories.

Then copy out these questions, and give each one the best reply. Choose from the list.
1 "What is the time, Tom?" asked Ann.
2 "How old are you, Kate?" asked Bob.
3 "Have you any pets Liz?" asked Colin.
4 "What are you doing, Steve?" asked Wendy.
5 "Are you in Miss Green's class?" asked Mike.

"I am looking for my hammer," replied Steve.
"I am eight," replied Kate.
"No, I'm in Miss Carter's class," replied Tommy.
"It is half past six," replied Tom.
"Yes, I have two hamsters," replied Liz.

C Brief conversation

There is one word missing from each of these brief conversations. *Write out the conversations and choose the missing word from the list.* Remember to copy the punctuation carefully.

mine   dragon   pullover
playing   fetch

"What do you think I am?" asked Ted.
"I think you must be a __," replied Ann.
"Leave my football alone!" shouted the boy.
"I'm sorry, I thought it was __," said Bob.
"I need the hammer," said Mr Wilson.
"I will __ it for you," said Tony.
"I can't find my slippers," said Wendy.
"I saw the dog __ with them a moment ago," said her Mother.
"I'm boiling hot!" exclaimed Peter.
"Why not take off your __, then?" said his father.

D Always, sometimes, never

Here are some questions that Miss Lee asked her pupils. What do you think they replied? *Write their replies as if you were writing a story.* Use <u>always</u>, <u>sometimes</u> or <u>never</u> in each reply.

You could begin like this:

"Do dogs ever swim, Bob?" asked Miss Lee.

"Yes, they sometimes do," replied Bob.

1 "Do dogs ever swim, Bob?" asked Miss Lee.
2 "Are footballs ever square, Tom?" asked Miss Lee.
3 "Is the sea always salt, Jo?" she asked.
4 "Do you ever drive a car, Ann?" she asked.
5 "Does water ever go solid?" asked Miss Lee.
6 "Are you ever punctual, Ted?" she asked.

E Something to write about

1 When I am on my way to school the first big building I pass is the library. It's on my right. Then I pass the Rex Cinema on my left. Just at the bend in the road I come to the indoor swimming pool on the right. A little farther on there is the Police Station on the right too . . .
Can you finish this for Kevin?
2 Write about what you pass every morning on your way to school.

F Something to find out

1 How long does it take you to get to school?
2 How long does it take a jet to cross the Atlantic from London to New York?
3 How long did it take the first airman who crossed the Atlantic?

4 How long did it take Magellan to sail round the world in 1519?
5 How long does it take the moon to go round the earth?

55

STEP 28

1 Sunday	2 Monday	3 Tuesday
4 Wednesday	5 Thursday	
6 Friday	7 Saturday	

A The weather

Let's pretend that the pictures show the sort of weather we had last week. *Write a sentence to say what the weather was like each day.* The words in the patch will help you. *Begin like this:*

1 On Sunday it was very misty.
2 On Monday . . .

B Write your own sentences

Write sentences to tell us:
1 what the weather is really like today
2 what the weather was like yesterday
3 what it was like on your birthday
4 what you hope it will be like for your holidays
5 what you think it is like at the North Pole

cloudy		frosty
windy	sunny	rained
misty		snowed

C Think it out

In how many ways are they the same, and in how many ways are they different? They are the same in one way and they are different in two ways. They are both apples. But the first is red and the second is green, and the first is smaller than the second.
Now say in how many ways the other pair are the same, and in how many ways they are different.

D Put the sentences in order

These sentences tell the story of the pictures. *Put them in the right order.*

Soon they came to the edge of a large lake.

His dog plunged into the water and swam to the stick.

Then he shook himself dry.

One day Kevin took his Golden Retriever for a walk.

He brought the stick back and laid it at Kevin's feet.

Kevin threw a stick into the lake.

E More sentences to make into a story

This time there are no pictures to help you put the sentences in order.

Just as he opened the front door, he heard people talking.

Tommy felt frightened.

He walked boldly into the lounge and found someone had left the television on.

Two strangers were having an angry argument.

One day Tommy came home to an empty house.

He was just going to run away, when he changed his mind.

F Another story

Here are some more pictures that tell
a story. *Try to tell the story in words.*
The words in the patch may help you.

Tom Thumb	kitchen	climbed
mother	fork	edge
bowl	dragged	balance
pudding	against	sticky

STEP 29

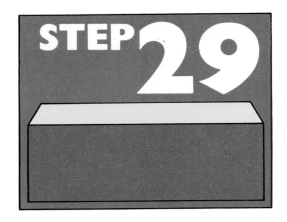

Kevin's uncle lives in Cornwall by the sea. He is a fisherman. He has a motor boat and catches fish with nets. In the summer he earns some extra money by using his boat to take holiday makers for trips along the coast.

Last year his uncle and aunt invited Kevin to spend a fortnight with them. When he got back home, Kevin wrote a 'thank you' letter to his uncle and aunt.

A Questions

1 To whom did Kevin write his letter?
2 On what date did he write it?
3 What is the number of Kevin's house?
4 In what town does he live?
5 In what county is Newtown?
6 Did he go fishing with his uncle?
7 What else did he do with his uncle?
8 Why hasn't Kevin told his mother about his aunt's cooking?

16 Lower Road,
Newtown,
Yorkshire.

28th August 1974

Dear Aunty and Uncle,

What a wonderful holiday you gave me! I enjoyed every moment of it. It was a dream holiday.

I specially remember the long fishing trip. It was very kind of you, Uncle, to take me with you. I enjoyed the trips along the coast too-every one of them. But even without them I should have had an unbeatable holiday just playing on the beach.

And the food! I haven't been able to tell Mum how good it all was, Aunty, in case she is jealous. Thank you both very very much.

Mum and Dad send their best wishes.

With love,
from
Kevin

B Addresses

This is how Kevin addressed the
envelope for his letter. *Draw
the shapes for five envelopes and then
address them to the following people:*

1 Mr D. Watson, 18 Tap Road, Hull, Yorks.
2 Mrs Carr, 5 Jay Street, Chard, Devon.
3 Dr P. Brown, 35 York Road, London, SW10.
4 Your head teacher at school.
5 Yourself.

Mr and Mrs Blake,
250 Hill Road,
FALMOUTH,
Cornwall.

C Map reading

Here is a special map. It is not like a map you find in an atlas, because it
has pictures of things of interest to see.
Pretend you started at the Old Barn and followed the arrows on the dotted
track and so came back to the Old Barn. *Describe the way you went and what you
saw. The pictures and their labels will of course help you.*

D A letter to write

Imagine that some relations or friends invited you to spend a holiday with them.
It can be anywhere in the world, and any sort of holiday. You had a glorious time.
*Write a 'thank you' letter like Kevin's. Remember to set the letter out carefully
as Kevin did.*

STEP 30

small

medium

big

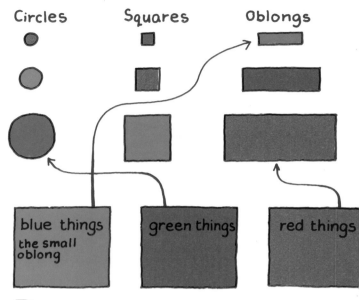

Circles   Squares   Oblongs

blue things
the small oblong

green things

red things

A Big, medium, small

Draw the three boxes and put in the headings. What are you going to write in each box? Which are the blue things? Well, the small oblong is blue. The medium circle is also blue, and so is the big square. So you write all three in the box marked *blue things*. Then you find the red things and write those in. Last of all you write in the names of the green things.

B Draw and write

Draw a big lorry, a medium lorry and a small lorry. Write under each what it is.

C Triangles

Do you know this shape? It's a triangle. Draw three triangles. Make one small, one medium and one big. Let the medium one be the same colour as this one. Then colour the small one green and the big one blue.
Write under each what it is, like this: *a big blue triangle.*

D They aren't, they are

Make six sentences to say what each shape is not. Then make a seventh to say what it is. Begin like this:

1 The first shape isn't red.
2 It isn't blue.
3 It isn't large.
4 It isn't medium.
5 It isn't a square.
6 It isn't an oblong.
7 It is a small green triangle.

E A word puzzle

Copy the puzzle and then write in the words:

			I				
1			I				
2			A				
3			O				
4				E			
5			E				
6	E						

1 It has three sides.
2 It has four equal sides.
3 It has 2 long and 2 short sides.
4 It is a round shape.
5 A triangle has only three.
6 Between big and small.

F A camera shot

We are looking down on Sue and Gary in this picture, as a tv camera sometimes does. Put yourself in Sue's shoes and think out what she can see. If you asked her what she can see, she might say:

I can see a lorry in front of me. Then there is a sack on my left and a crate on my right.

What would Gary say?

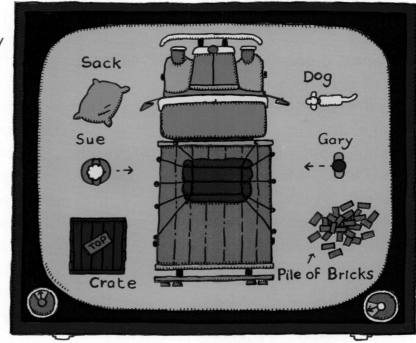

G Timothy Jones

This is a kind of joke poem. The joke is Timothy's impossible action. What did he do that was impossible, and why was it impossible?

Timothy Jones
Liked a dinner of bones,
And for tea he would choose
A pair of old shoes.

His teeth grew so long,
So sharp and so strong,
That he bit off his face,
Leaving only a space.
Ruth Ainsworth

H Something to write

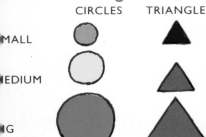

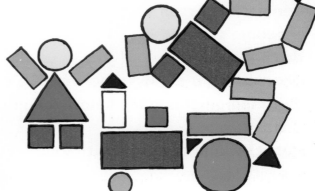

The lady is made up of a circle, a triangle, two squares and two oblongs. The head is a medium circle. The body is a large triangle. The arms are small oblongs, and the legs are medium squares.
Now describe the puppet and the tractor in the same way.

acrobat, a person who does clever things on tight ropes, trapezes, etc.

airport, a place where aircraft land or take off

angler, a person who catches fish with a rod and line

ascend, to go up or to climb

bakery, a place where bread is made

banjo, a musical instrument with strings that are plucked

bluntly, plainly

boast, to praise oneself too much

bricklayer, a person who lays bricks

butcher, a person who cuts up and sells meat

camera, a machine for taking photos

cemetery, a place where the dead are buried

century, a hundred years

chatter, to talk quickly and without much meaning

circle, a round shape

convinced, able to believe

crestfallen, upset

dentist, a person who looks after people's teeth

dozen, twelve

dramatist, a person who writes plays

dwarf, a person much below the normal size

egret, a kind of heron with long feathers in its tail

encore, what you say at the end if you want the actors to do it again

faint, to lose one's senses for a short time

fiddler, a person who plays the violin

florist, a person who sells flowers

fluff, the soft feathery stuff that comes from blankets

forsake, to break away from or desert

groom, a person who is paid to look after horses

idly, not doing anything

igloo, a kind of house built of snow

imprison, to put in prison

injure, to hurt or damage

juggle, to do tricks with things like plate or balls to amuse people

kayak, a kind of light canoe used by Eskimos

laundry, a building where clothes are washed and pressed

mallet, a hammer with a wooden head

medium, between large and small

motorist, a person who drives a motor ca

nest, a place made by a bird for its eggs

oblong, a shape with two long and two short sides

orchard, a field where apples are grown

pianist, a person who plays the piano

plough, an implement for turning over the soil

plump, fat and chubby

poacher, a person who steals animals from someone else's land

potter, a person who makes pots from clay

prison, a building where criminals are kept

puzzled, left wondering

quartet, a group of four musicians

razor, an instrument to shave with

restaurant, a place where meals can be bought and eaten

cald, to hurt with hot liquid

core, twenty

hears, a tool for cutting hedges

ide, one of the lines that make the edge of a shape like a square or triangle

pectator, a person who watches a game or contest

quare, a shape with four equal sides

tationer, a person who sells writing paper, envelopes, pencils, etc.

tream, a small river

urgeon, a doctor who performs operations

theatre, a building where plays are performed

tight, the opposite of *loose*

triangle, a shape with three sides

trio, a group of three

umpire, a person who acts as the judge in certain games like tennis or cricket.

upset, to tip over or overturn

walrus, a large sea-animal with two long tusks

wardrobe, a cupboard where clothes are kept

widow, a woman who has lost her husband

xylophone, a musical instrument with wooden bars to be struck

zip, a fastener with metal teeth that lock together

Acknowledgements

We are grateful to the following for permission to reproduce copyright material:

Author's Agents for an extract from the poem 'Stop-Go' by Dorothy W. Baruch from *Childcraft Vol. 1*. Permission granted by Bertha Klausner International Literary Agency Inc; A. & C. Black Ltd. for an extract from the poem 'The Dustman' from *Speech Rhymes* by Clive Sansom, published by A. & C. Black Ltd; The Author and Evans Bros. Books Ltd. for an extract from the poem 'Flying' by J. M. Westrup. Published by Evans Bros. Books Ltd. and the Author and Heinemann Educational Books Ltd. for an extract from the poem 'Timothy Jones' by Ruth Ainsworth from *Look Ahead Readers Book 4*, published by Heinemann Educational Books Ltd.